BOATING BASICS

by

Henry F. Halsted

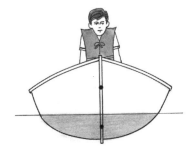

Illustrated by
Art Seiden

With Photographs

Created and Produced by
Arvid Knudsen

Prentice-Hall, Inc.
Englewood Cliffs, New Jersey

Other **Sports Basics Books** in Series

BASKETBALL BASICS *by Greggory Morris*
RUNNING BASICS *by Carol Lea Benjamin*
DISCO BASICS *by Maxine Polley*
GYMNASTICS BASICS *by John and Mary Jean Traetta*
RACQUETBALL BASICS *by Tony Boccaccio*
FRISBEE DISC BASICS *by Dan Roddick*
SWIMMING BASICS *by Rob Orr and Jane B. Tyler*
HORSEBACK RIDING BASICS *by Dianne Reimer*
SKIING BASICS *by Al Morrozzi*
BASEBALL BASICS *by Jack Lang*
FISHING BASICS *by John Randolph*
FOOTBALL BASICS *by Larry Fox*
SOCCER BASICS *by Alex Yannis*
SAILING BASICS *by Lorna Slocombe*
BICYCLING BASICS *by Tim and Glenda Wilhelm*
BACKPACKING BASICS *by John Randolph*
TENNIS BASICS *by Robert J. LaMarche*
TRACK & FIELD BASICS *by Fred McMane*
HOCKEY BASICS *by Norman MacLean*
BOWLING BASICS *by Chuck Pezzano*
KARATE BASICS *by Thomas J. Nardi*
ICE-SKATING BASICS *by Norman MacLean*
WATERSPORTS BASICS *by Don Wallace*
CAMPING BASICS *by Wayne Armstrong*

Text copyright © 1985 by Henry F. Halsted and Arvid Knudsen
Illustrations copyright © 1985 by Arvid Knudsen

Book design by Arvid Knudsen

Printed in the United States of America   · J

Prentice-Hall International (UK) Limited, London
Prentice-Hall of Australia, Pty. Ltd., Sydney
Prentice-Hall Canada, Inc., Toronto
Prentice-Hall Hispanoamericana, S.A., Mexico
Prentice-Hall of India Private Ltd., New Delhi
Prentice-Hall of Japan, Inc., Tokyo
Prentice-Hall of Southeast Asia Pte. Ltd., Singapore
Whitehall Books Limited, Wellington, New Zealand
Editora Prentice-Hall do Brasil Ltda., Rio de Janeiro

10 9 8 7 6 5 4 3 2 1

Library of Congress Cataloging in Publication Data

Halsted, Henry F.
    Boating basics.

    Summary: Describes various types of small boats and what makes them float and move. Also discusses techniques of paddling and rowing, using outboard motors, and safety tips.
    1. Boats and boating—Juvenile literature.
[1. Boats and boating]   I. Seiden, Art, ill.
II. Knudsen, Arvid.   III. Title.
GV775.7.H32   1985   797.1   85-9406
ISBN 0-13-078502-4

CONTENTS

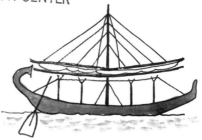

ANCIENT EGYPTIAN SHIP - 1500 BC

1 / Beginnings

The history of boating dates almost as far into the past as does the history of mankind. From the beginning, boats and man developed in an amazingly parallel pattern. As man became more advanced in creating and using tools, his boats became more advanced, which in turn expanded his horizons for fishing, trade, and exploration. The farther our ancestors traveled, the more they came in touch with other cultures —learning about their tools and techniques for boat construction and navigation. This, in turn, farther expanded the horizons at sea.

The development of boats by prehistoric man is not part of recorded history, but it must have followed a logical pattern. Our ancestors probably first took to the water of necessity—either to gather food for their family or perhaps to avoid being eaten by a prehistoric animal. The first "boat" was undoubtedly a log that an ancestral swimmer held onto in order to help him remain afloat.

Once he discovered that logs could be used as floats, man probably continued to use them in this manner, holding on to stay afloat while swimming into deeper water. The next step may have been sitting astride the log, paddling about with his hands. At some point, someone climbed aboard several logs that were tangled together and discovered that in this arrangement the logs were much less tippy. This was the birth of the raft. Logs were tied together with vines or strips of animal hide, which created a stable platform to carry one or a number of people about on the water.

5

Photo by Arvid Knudsen.

Man used poles to push himself from one place to another while aboard his rafts in shallow water. When he strayed into deeper water where the pole could no longer reach bottom, he accidentally discovered how to paddle, repeatedly pulling the pole through the water in an effort to return to shore. Seeing that this worked, it was only natural to seek out poles with flat surfaces at the base, which worked better for paddling. Modern paddles and oars are the present-day descendants of these original flat-bottomed poles.

Discovery of the Dugout Canoe

While experimenting with log boats and rafts, at one point the prehistoric boatmen may have come across a log that had been struck by lightning and hollowed out. When they tried floating on the log, they noticed that it was lighter and easier to handle than others. From this probable beginning came the dugout canoe. Our ancestors began burning out logs, then scraping them out with any tools they had at hand. As tools became more refined, so did the dugout canoes.

Dugout canoes developed during the same time period in many different parts of the world. The characteristics of the canoes varied according to the type of trees available. Small, simple dugout canoes were used from Africa to South America and by a number of the Indian tribes inhabiting the Eastern Seaboard of North America. In many areas, the dugout canoes became much larger and elaborate. In Florida, the Seminole Indians developed a long and graceful canoe, as did some of the tribes in Central America. American Indians in the Pacific Northwest built huge canoes of cedar trees, some as long as sixty feet, for use on the ocean. In the South Pacific Ocean, Polynesian tribes built large war canoes with outriggers, on which they were known to travel several thousand miles at sea.

As canoes developed in Egypt and Phoenicia, planks were added along the top edge of the craft to make them higher above the water. This kept spray and waves out of the canoe while providing more buoyancy and allowing greater loads to be carried in the craft. As building techniques improved, more and more boards were added, both above and below the waterline, until the only thing remaining of the solid wood canoe was the keel, or backbone of the boat.

The Galley—First of the Modern Boats

The keel and planking system is the foundation of modern boat-building. Some of the first boats of this type were the galleys, wood-planked boats and ships used by the ancient Egyptians, Phoenicians, Greeks, and Romans, dating from about 3000 B.C. It was aboard these vessels that rowing as we know it came into existence. The galleys were propelled by rows of oars on both sides of the craft, each oar tended by one or more men, usually slaves. Galleys also were some of the first boats to use sails, which they set when traveling downwind.

Steam Power and Modern Boats

A number of advances were made in boat design and sail power by European countries during the age of exploration when Magellan, Columbus, and Captain Cook were making their famous voyages. The next great discovery was made by an American named John Fitch. In 1788 he developed the first steam-powered vessel. By the mid-1800s, steam-powered boats were a common sight both on inland rivers and far at sea. Following the steamers came the steam turbines, then diesel- and gasoline-powered boats.

In more recent times, we have learned how to build boats of new materials such as steel, aluminum, and fiberglass. Advances in engineering have created lighter, stronger, and more seaworthy craft, capable of greater speeds and massive load-carrying capability. These new techniques and materials have carried over into small boats such as aluminum canoes, rowboats, and runabouts. There have been great advances in small sailboats as well, which allow them to sail very closely into the wind and quite fast when sailing downwind.

Modern small boats also have become relatively inexpensive, so the use of pleasure boats has become very popular. Rowing, canoeing, sailing, and small outboards are being used worldwide. Everywhere, people are out having fun on the water.

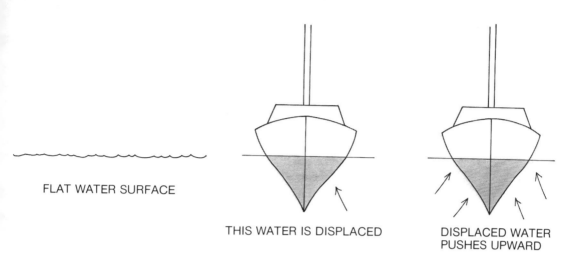

FLAT WATER SURFACE

THIS WATER IS DISPLACED

DISPLACED WATER
PUSHES UPWARD

2 / What Makes Boats Float?

The principle of buoyancy was discovered by Archimedes in about 225 B.C. Obviously, boats had been in use for thousands of years before that time, but it was Archimedes who discovered the principle that keeps boats afloat.

Archimedes [AR kuh ME deez) knew that the natural state of the surface of water or any liquid is to remain flat. When a boat floats in the water, it displaces, or pushes some of the water aside. The tendency of the water surrounding the boat is to rush back in toward the displaced water, which creates an upward force against the boat that holds it on the surface of the water. Part of Archimedes Principle says that the buoyancy, or upward force, is equal to the weight of the water that is pushed aside by the area of the boat that is under water.

Beach Balls Float—How About Wood or Iron?

A cubic foot of water weighs sixty-four pounds. Therefore, if you had a beach ball in the shape of a one-foot cube, you would have to push down with a force of sixty-four pounds to hold the cube under water. We all know that beach balls float. How about a block of wood? Usually wood floats, and it will always float as long as it weighs less than sixty-four pounds to a cubic foot. If a cubic-foot block of wood weighs thirty-two pounds, or half as much as water, it will float with only half the block under water.

Photo by Arvid Knudsen.

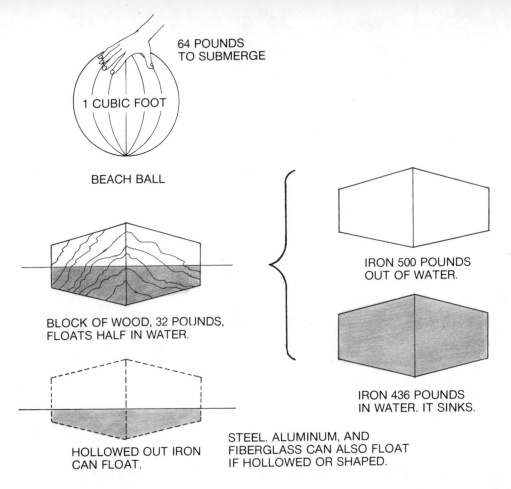

64 POUNDS
TO SUBMERGE

1 CUBIC FOOT

BEACH BALL

BLOCK OF WOOD, 32 POUNDS,
FLOATS HALF IN WATER.

IRON 500 POUNDS
OUT OF WATER.

IRON 436 POUNDS
IN WATER. IT SINKS.

HOLLOWED OUT IRON
CAN FLOAT.

STEEL. ALUMINUM, AND
FIBERGLASS CAN ALSO FLOAT
IF HOLLOWED OR SHAPED.

But boats are made of iron and steel. How do they float? A cubic foot of iron weighs almost 500 pounds. If you put that block in the water, it will surely sink straight to the bottom. But still Archimedes Principle works. The displaced water still pushes the iron upward with a force of sixty-four pounds; so in the water, the iron weighs about 436 pounds. In order to make a cube of iron float, it has to be hollowed out until it weighs less than sixty-four pounds to a cubic foot.

This is the principle that keeps boats afloat. The water that is displaced by the boat weighs the same as the total weight of the boat. Buoyancy pushes the boat upward with the same force as its weight. The boat will float as long as it weighs less than the water it displaces.

Along with iron and steel, many modern boat-building materials, such as fiberglass and aluminum, are heavier than water when they are in solid blocks. Therefore, the materials must be hollowed out or shaped into a form that is lighter than water. As long as these boats are on top of the water, the principle of buoyancy will keep them afloat. But if these boats leak or are allowed to fill up with water, they may loose their buoyancy and sink to the bottom. This is why we must be very careful to keep boats from tipping over and to *bail*, or pump out, any water that leaks into the boat.

Keeping Boats in Proper Trim

The very center of the boat's shape under water is called the *center of buoyancy*. This is the center point where the force of water pushing up is focused. The center of buoyancy is controlled by the shape and weight of the boat. The middle point of all the boat's weight is called the *center of gravity*. This is the main point where the boat's downward force is centered. The way these two centers balance against each other determines how the boat will float.

If most of the weight of the boat and its passengers is located at the back, or *stern*, of the boat, then it will float with the front, or *bow*, up out of the water. If most of the weight is toward the bow, then the stern will be too high. Balancing the weight in the boat is called keeping it in proper *trim*. For proper trim, you must arrange the weight in the boat so the center of gravity moves back to the middle of the boat. This is true both for front and back (*fore* and *aft*) trim and for side-to-side (*athwartship*) trim as well. If the center of gravity gets too far over to the side of the boat, it will tip right over.

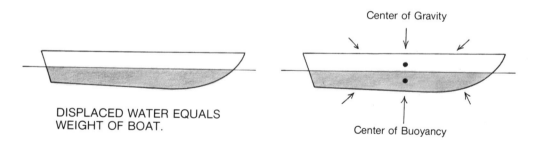

DISPLACED WATER EQUALS
WEIGHT OF BOAT.

Center of Gravity

Center of Buoyancy

Keep Low in the Boat

Another very important relationship between the center of gravity and the center of buoyancy has to do with how far they are apart. If the weight is kept very low in the boat, both centers will be very close to-

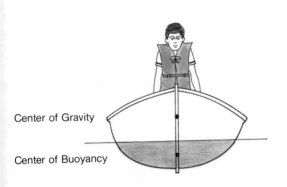
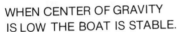

Center of Gravity

Center of Buoyancy

WHEN CENTER OF GRAVITY
IS LOW THE BOAT IS STABLE.

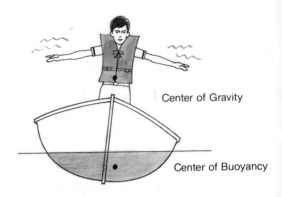

Center of Gravity

Center of Buoyancy

WHEN CENTER OF GRAVITY
IS HIGH BOAT IS TIPPY.

gether, which keeps the boat very stable. But the farther the two centers are apart, the tippier the boat gets, making it very easy to capsize. This is the reason why it is so important always to sit down in the boat. Standing up in a small boat is dangerous because when you stand up, you raise the center of gravity, which could cause the boat to tip over.

You can have lots of fun out on the water aboard small boats, but it is important to understand the rules of buoyancy. These rules are the same whether you are in a rowboat, a canoe, a sailboat, or an outboard runabout. But as we will see, each type of boat is a little different.

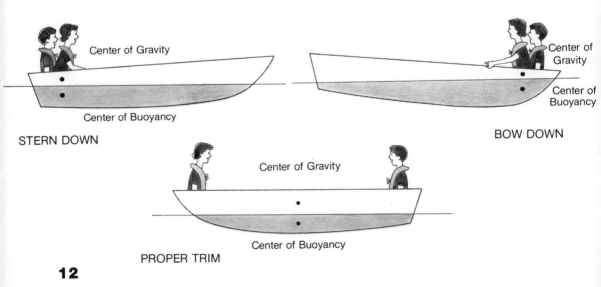

Center of Gravity

Center of Buoyancy

STERN DOWN

Center of
Gravity

Center of
Buoyancy

BOW DOWN

Center of Gravity

Center of Buoyancy

PROPER TRIM

12

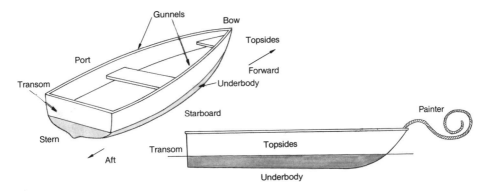

3 / The Language of Boats

As you begin to learn about boats, you will notice that there are parts that have interesting names. This will seem almost as if you are learning a new language at first. But as you spend more time on the water you will become familiar with the language of boating.

First of all, aboard boats there is no such thing as left and right. The left side of a boat is called the *port* side, and the right side is called the *starboard* side. Although this may seem strange at first, it is for a good reason. If you were in the back seat of the boat facing forward and your friend was in the front seat facing back, your right and left sides would be opposite. If someone said "lean to your right," you would lean to opposite sides. Aboard boats, there is only one port side and one starboard side. If someone said "lean to the port side," you and your friend would both lean the same way.

The back of the boat is called the *stern* (sometimes it is called the *aft* end). Moving toward the stern is called *moving aft*. The square section at the very back of a boat is called the *transom*. The front of the boat is called the *bow*, or the forward end. Moving toward the bow is called *moving forward*. That's easy to remember.

The part of the boat that is under water is called the *underbody*. The part above water is called the *topsides*. The very top edge of the boat along both sides are the *gunnels*.

Finally, the line you use to tie up the boat is called the *painter*. (I wonder how it got that name.)

These names are the same for all boats. Of course, as we learn more about the different kinds of boats, we'll learn some new names as well.

14

4 / Canoes

Canoes have more uses than almost any other type of boat. Not only are they fun to paddle around in, but they are light enough to carry almost anywhere. When the early explorers paddled all the way to the head of a river, they could just walk overland and carry, or *portage*, the canoes until they reached another body of water. Also, because they are so light, canoes can be floated in very shallow water. Although they usually are used in calm water, if they are handled by experts they are very seaworthy and can safely navigate wild rapids and very choppy seas. Whether they are used for fishing, transportation, sport, or just paddling around, canoes are truly the magic carpets of the boating world.

Come Aboard But Step Carefully!

The most important thing to remember about canoes is that because they are quite narrow, they also can be very tippy. They don't really require good balance—anybody can paddle a canoe. You just have to remember always to keep your weight low and toward the center of the canoe.

Keep this in mind as you get aboard. Climbing into the canoe from a dock, start by crouching down and steadying the canoe with one hand on the gunnel, or top edge, of the canoe. Keep your fingers pointed inside the boat so they don't get pinched between the canoe and the dock. Now, reach out with one leg and set it lightly in the center of the canoe, then gradually shift your weight onto that leg. As you enter the canoe, reach your other hand across to the far gunnel, then sit down on the seat. Now you are afloat!

Once you are seated in the canoe, rock side to side gently to get a feel for how the boat responds. You'll find that as long as you sit down and keep your weight low, canoes are really pretty stable.

The Basic Forward Stroke

Start out by learning to paddle on your strongest side. If you are right-handed, paddle on your right side. If you are a lefty, start by paddling on your left.

Grasp the paddle with your stronger hand just above the blade and place your other hand on the handle at the top. You will notice that the handle is designed to fit nicely into the palm of your hand. The wide grip is comfortable to push against during the stroke and it

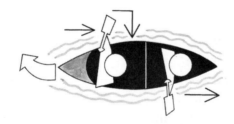

CANOE HAS NATURAL TENDENCY TO VEER AWAY FROM STERN PADDLER'S SIDE.

STERN PRY CORRECTS BY PUSHING THE STERN BACK INTO LINE.

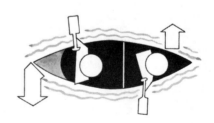

also is handy for steering the paddle through the water. The stroke involves pushing the paddle with your upper hand while you pull the blade against the water with your lower hand.

Begin the stroke by reaching forward with your lower hand and upper body. The upper hand should be a little bit in front of your shoulders. The power stroke begins at the forward part of your reach. Put the paddle into the water to the upper edge of the blade, then pull back with your lower hand as you push ahead with your upper hand.

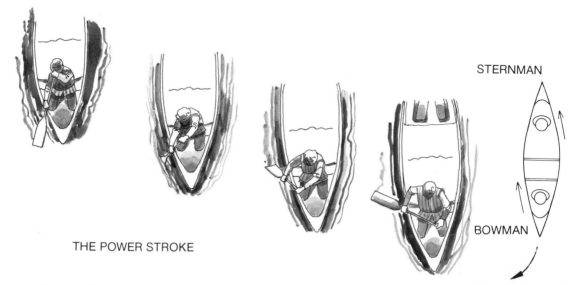

STERNMAN

BOWMAN

THE POWER STROKE

Remember, the upper hand also steers the paddle parallel to the canoe. Continue the power stroke until the blade is about even with your hip, then relax the pressure on both arms and the paddle will come to the surface of the water automatically. Next, lift the blade clear of the water and reach forward for the return part of the stroke. That's all there is to it.

Steering a Canoe

If you always paddle with standard strokes on only one side of the canoe, it won't go straight. Instead, it will go in circles. That's fun to try sometimes, but if you want to get anywhere you'll have to learn how to steer.

Usually, canoes are paddled by two people, one on each side. This is very helpful to keep the canoe going straight, but still it must be controlled with alternate strokes.

THE STERN PRY

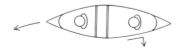

As two people paddle a canoe, the person in the stern has more control over the steering. Because he is paddling from the position where the canoe is more easily controlled, after a few strokes the canoe will begin to turn away from the side the sternman is paddling on. The easiest stroke that can be used to correct this effect is called the *stern pry*. Every few strokes, or whenever it is needed, the sternman should continue his stroke until the paddle is well behind him, then pull the paddle into the gunnel with his lower hand and hold it there. Next, using the upper hand, pull in toward the canoe, to use the paddle as a rudder and "pry" the canoe back on course. The stern pry also can be used when paddling alone in a canoe, to keep it going straight while you paddle on only one side.

The Stern Sweep

When you want to move the stern toward the side you are paddling on, use the *stern sweep* stroke. For this stroke, the sternman reaches out from his shoulder and paddles in a small arc back in toward the canoe. This will turn the bow away from the side he is paddling on. When you are learning the stern sweep, be careful not to lean out too far and tip the canoe. But at the same time, don't be too timid. The stern sweep is a very effective steering stroke and also a good exercise in balance.

THE STERN SWEEP

THE STERN SWEEP BEGINS WELL AWAY FROM THE CANOE AND GETS ITS TOP POWER AS THE BLADE IS PULLED TOWARD THE STERN.

The J Stroke

The *J* stroke is very much like the stern pry, but it requires lots of practice to get it right. It is used by the stern paddler to keep the canoe going straight and also when paddling alone. Start the stroke just like the normal forward stroke, but when the paddle gets back even with your hip, use your upper hand to turn the inside blade toward the stern of the canoe. Then, pushing down with your upper hand and lifting with your lower hand, pry the paddle back up toward the water surface. This causes a sweeping motion, like a *J*, with the paddle that keeps the canoe going straight.

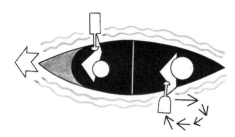

THE "J" STROKE

Both the *J* stroke and the stern pry are very effective when one person is in the canoe. For solo paddling, kneel just behind the center of the canoe to keep it in good trim. Paddling on only one side, you can use either the *J* stroke or the stern pry to keep the canoe on course. Another way to keep the canoe going straight is to alternate your strokes, paddling first on one side, then the other.

These are the basic strokes for steering and paddling canoes. As you practice and gain experience you will learn others. Canoes are great fun just for paddling around on the water and to get out to good fishing grounds. They are also excellent transportation on camping trips into remote areas. And "shooting the rapids" in a whitewater canoe is one of the most exciting sports on the water.

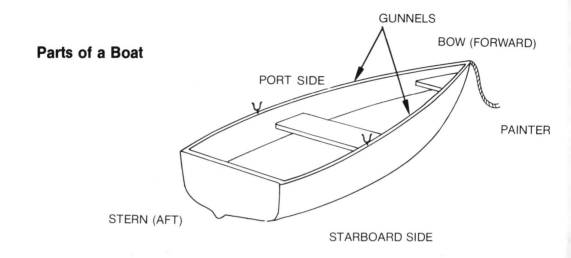

Parts of a Boat

GUNNELS

BOW (FORWARD)

PORT SIDE

PAINTER

STERN (AFT)

STARBOARD SIDE

5 / Rowboats

The principles of rowing are really quite simple. Basically, the oars are used like levers, pulling against the water to move the boat forward. The oars pivot at the gunnel, or top edge, of each side of the boat. They are held in position by *oarlocks*, U-shaped fittings that hold the oars in place but allow them to pivot. The tip of each oar is dipped into the water at the same time, pulled through the water, then lifted back clear of the water at the end of the stroke.

Rowing does take some getting used to, mostly because when you start it will seem as if everything is backward. You even sit facing the back of the boat. When you push down on the oar handles, the tips go up and out of the water. When you push the oar handles toward the back of the boat, the tips go forward—toward the front of the boat. All this may seem very confusing, but once you give it a try you will see that rowing is really easy to learn.

Getting Acquainted

Most small rowboats and prams have three seats: one in the bow, one near the center of the boat, and one in the stern. The rowing station is usually at the center seat, with oarlocks attached to the gunnels (top) on both sides of the boat and just a little behind the seat.

21

Photo courtesy of The Record.

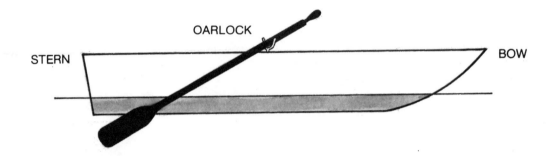

OARLOCK

STERN   BOW

Oars are anywhere from five feet long, for small rowboats, to over twelve feet on some racing shells. Almost all oars are still being built of wood. The inside end, from the oarlock to the handle, is called the *loom*. The part of the oar that rests in the oarlock usually is covered with leather to protect the wood from becoming frayed as it rubs, or *chafes*, against the oarlock. Outside the oarlock and beyond the leather *chafeguard*, the round part of the oar continues, making the *shaft* of the oar. At the base of the shaft the oar flattens out into the *blade*. The outside edge of the oar is called the *tip*.

Getting Comfortable

Start your rowing lesson by sitting at the center seat. Install both oarlocks in their sleeves, then rest each oar in its oarlock, with the protective leather centered in the oarlock. The oars are designed so that when the oars are properly centered with the leathers in the oarlocks, the handles will be close together in front of the rower. Rest your hands on the handles and try pushing them down at the same time. You will notice that the tips of the oars lift out of the water. Gripping the handles, rotate the oars and notice how the blades turn from parallel to square to the water. With the blades parallel to the water, push the handles out in front of you (toward the back of the boat) and notice that the blades move toward the front of the boat. Continue experimenting with the oars until you feel comfortable and can move them both at the same time, smoothly.

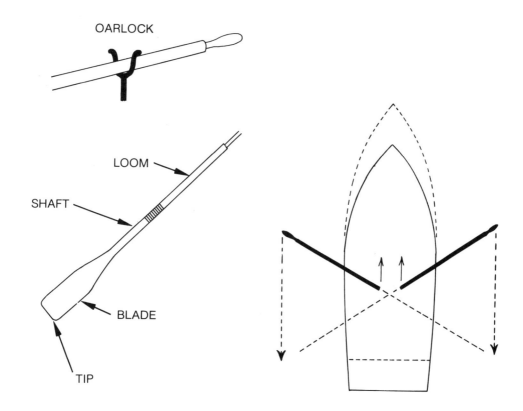

OARLOCK

LOOM

SHAFT

BLADE

TIP

Getting Underway

Once you are used to the way oars work, you are ready to begin rowing. Line up the oar blades so they are square to the water, then push down on the handles to lift the blades clear. Push the handles forward (toward the back of the boat) with your arms and upper body. This moves the blades toward the bow of the boat. From this position you are ready to begin the stroke. Raise the handles until the blades are in the water, still square with the edges up and down, then pull against the handles. You will notice the boat begin to move forward as you move the handles back toward your chest. When the oar blades begin to angle aft, ease up on the stroke and begin pushing down on the handles to lift the oars clear of the water, ending the power stroke. Again, push forward with your upper body and arms for the return part of the stroke, then drop the blades into the water for another stroke. Rowing is merely a process of repeating this over and over.

Feathering Your Oars

Once you are comfortable with the basic rowing stroke, try "feathering" the oar on the return part of the stroke. *Feathering the oar* means turning the oar a little during the return stroke so the blade doesn't splash or dig in if it hits small waves. At the end of the power stroke, when you are beginning the return part of the stroke, rotate the oar a little by dropping your wrists and rolling your thumbs away from your chest. Keep the oar blade angled like this until you have reached the end of the return stroke, then turn the oar back square to the water before beginning the power stroke.

Steering, Stopping, and Backing Up

Small rowboats don't have rudders so steering has to be done with the oars. The easiest way to turn the boat is to row on only one side of the boat—it will turn away from the side you stroke on. To get used to turning, row on one side until the boat turns around in a complete circle. Then try turning around the other way by rowing with the other oar. For small adjustments to your direction you can just pull harder on one side than the other when you are rowing forward.

One of the hardest things about rowing is seeing where you are going, because you face backward in the rowing seat. When rowing alone, you have to look back over your shoulder about once a minute to make sure you are going in the right direction. When there is a passenger in the aft seat, he or she can function as your lookout, telling you when you should adjust your course one way or the other.

The best way to stop quickly is to put both oars in the water at the same time and push against them. The drag they cause will work just like brakes and slow the boat down.

It is fun and easy to row a boat backward. All you have to do is reverse the stroke. Square the oars and put the blades in the water when they are angled toward the back of the boat, then push on the handles to move the boat backward. Raise the blades out of the water when they angle toward the bow of the boat and repeat the stroke to continue in reverse.

Advanced Strokes

You can turn the boat around quickly by rowing forward with one oar and backward with the other oar. This requires a good deal of practice because you have to pull on one oar while you push on the other. With practice though, you will learn complete control of the oars.

A different method of rowing forward involves alternating the strokes from side to side. Start by taking a stroke with the port oar, then take one with the starboard oar, then again with the port oar, and so on. When you can alternate your strokes smoothly, you will have mastered another technique of rowing.

Try rowing with one person in charge of each oar! Both rowers sit side by side at the center seat and grasp the handle of their oar with both hands. Then, try to begin and end each stroke at the same time. At first it will seem really funny as you get used to timing your stroke the same as your partner's. But as you learn how to adjust your rowing to the strength and timing of your partner, the boat will begin to move forward smoothly, as if only one person was rowing.

Row Safely and Have a Good Time!

As you are learning to row, always head *upwind* until you are confident that you will be able to row against the wind. Then if you get tired, the wind will help you get back to the dock. If you row on a river, row upstream first as you are learning. Like the wind, the current will help you get back when you are tired.

Rowing is not only lots of fun and a great way to get around on the water, but it is good exercise as well. As you become more advanced you may want to try some of the sleeker rowing boats. Perhaps someday you'll try a rowing shell with a sliding seat for more leg power, outriggers, and very long "spoon" oars. These boats can be rowed very fast—faster than some outboard runabouts.

Photo courtesy of The Record.

6 / Sailing

It is easy to understand how boats sail *downwind*. Just as you can feel how the wind helps to move you along when you are riding your bike or skating with the wind behind you, you can feel a sailboat as it goes downwind. The wind just pushes it along.

It is a little harder to understand how sailboats sail across the wind, and sometimes almost into the wind. This is possible because all sailboats have a *centerboard*, or *keel*, on the bottom that keeps them from being blown sideways by the breeze. When sailing across the wind, the force on the sail pushes them forward and the centerboard keeps them from slipping downwind. The centerboard actually is very effective in keeping the boat going forward, so much so that the sail can be trimmed in almost to the middle of the boat when the boat sails to *windward* (into the wind). With wind pushing on the sail and the centerboard keeping it from going sideways, the boat is forced to move ahead. It's the same as when you squeeze a watermelon seed between your fingers and it shoots forward because of the opposing pressures.

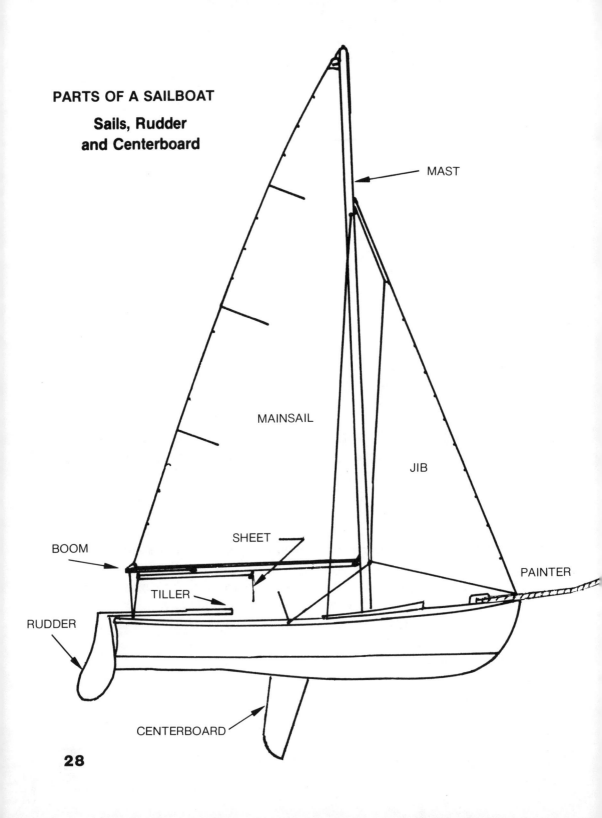

PARTS OF A SAILBOAT

**Sails, Rudder
and Centerboard**

MAST

MAINSAIL

JIB

SHEET

BOOM

PAINTER

TILLER

RUDDER

CENTERBOARD

Getting to Know the Boat

It is important to know the names for the different parts of the sail-boat. Even the easiest things have names that are different from what you would expect.

The *rudder* is what steers the boat. But when you are sailing, you don't hold onto the rudder. There is a pole, or lever, that comes forward from the rudder, which is called the *tiller*. The stern of the boat steers toward the direction in which you push the tiller.

The sail is held up on the *mast* and hauled outward on the *boom*, a pole that comes backward from the mast about three feet up from the deck. (I don't know why they named it the boom—maybe it's because if you don't duck your head when the sail comes across the boat, it will "boom" you in the head. So every time you *tack* over, from one direction to the other, be sure to duck!)

The boom and the sail are controlled by a line called the *sheet*. When the boat sails into the wind, you pull in the sheet to move the sail in close to the boat. When you sail downwind, you let out, or *slack the sheet*, to let the sail out as far as possible.

When the sail is facing into the wind, it will flap around like a flag. This is called *luffing*. When the boat is sailing a little too close to the wind, luffing first begins at the forward edge of the sail, and it is a sign that the sheet should be pulled in to trim the sail.

Know the Wind

The most important factor to be aware of when you are sailing is where the wind is coming from. Seasoned sailors can sense the wind and how it is oriented to their boats. Usually, you can see where the wind is coming from by checking the waves. They are usually caused by wind and come from the same direction. Another good test is to wet your finger and hold it up to the breeze. The side that gets coldest is the side the wind is coming from. You can also find where the wind is coming from by facing into the breeze. When the breeze feels the same on both cheeks and sounds the same in both ears, you are looking directly upwind.

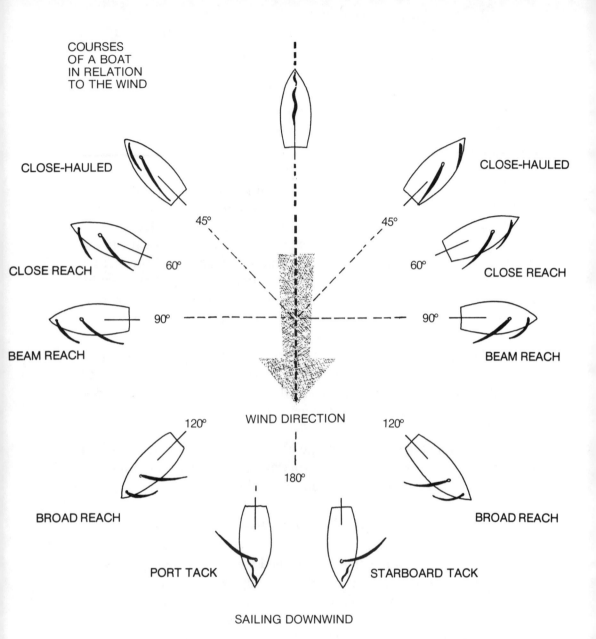

COURSES
OF A BOAT
IN RELATION
TO THE WIND

CLOSE-HAULED

CLOSE-HAULED

45°

45°

CLOSE REACH

60°

60°

CLOSE REACH

90°

90°

BEAM REACH

BEAM REACH

120°

WIND DIRECTION

120°

180°

BROAD REACH

BROAD REACH

PORT TACK

STARBOARD TACK

SAILING DOWNWIND

Everything in sailing is done according to the wind. The boat is either sailing closehauled into the wind with the sail trimmed in tight, "reaching" across the wind with the sail let out a little, or "running" downwind with the sail let out all the way.

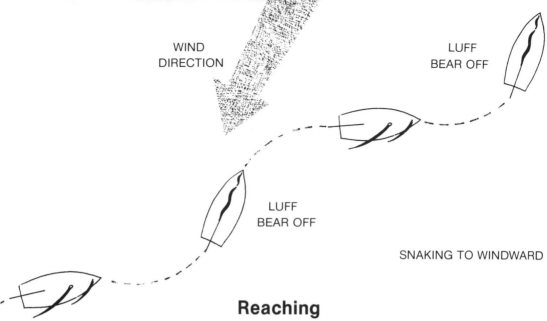

WIND
DIRECTION

LUFF
BEAR OFF

LUFF
BEAR OFF

SNAKING TO WINDWARD

Reaching

The easiest point of sail to start with is reaching. Point the boat across the wind, parallel to the waves, and trim the sail in about half way. The first thing you will notice as the boat begins to move forward is that it will also tip, or *heel*, to the downwind, *leeward*, side. Don't be alarmed! All sailboats heel to leeward. To keep the boat as level as possible, sit to the upwind, *windward*, side. If the wind picks up and the boat starts to heel too much, all you have to do is let out the main sheet until the wind spills out of the sail and it begins to luff. Try this a couple of times until you feel comfortable sailing with the boat heeled over.

When you are confident in reaching across the wind, you can try changing course either to sail closer to the wind, *close reaching*, or to sail farther downwind, or *broad reaching*. Changing course to sail closer to the wind is called *heading up*. As you push the tiller toward the downwind side of the boat, you will notice that the sail begins to luff at the forward edge. To stop the luffing, pull the sail in a little by *trimming the sheet*.

Changing course to sail farther downwind is called *bearing off*. Pull the tiller a little toward the windward side of the boat to steer her more downwind and "ease the sheet out" to keep as much wind in the sail as possible. If you let the sail out too much, it will begin to luff, so pull it back in again until it is full. On most boats, reaching is the fastest point of sail. It is fun to set the sails perfectly and really see how fast the boat can go!

Sailing Closehauled

Next, try sailing *closehauled*. This involves sailing the boat as close to the wind as possible. Pull in the sheet until the sail is just over the downwind side of the boat and leave it set there. The rest of the adjustments as you sail to windward will be made by steering with the tiller. Steer up into the wind until the sail begins to luff a little. This time don't trim the sheet to stop the luff but pull the tiller back to windward a bit and bear off just until the luffing stops. As you sail to windward, keep trying to sail a little higher until the luff appears, then bear off again. This is often called *snaking to weather* because the motion is a little like a snake. You gradually sail up into the wind until the sail luffs, then bear off a little to keep the sail full. Sailing to weather requires lots of concentration, but it is one of the most fun points of sail. This is where you can really get in tune with the sailboat.

SAILBOATS SAIL INTO THE WIND
BY "TACKING", ZIGZAGGING, UPWIND.

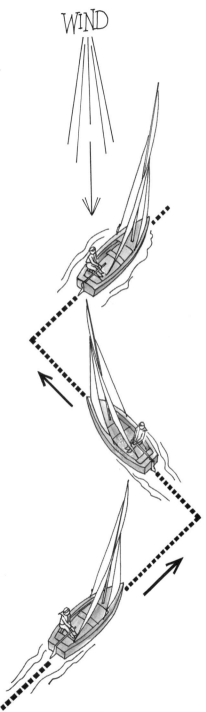

WIND

Changing Direction: Coming About and Gybing

Once you have mastered reaching and sailing closehauled, it is time to learn how to *come about,* by steering the bow across the wind on to the other tack. This is the way boats sail into the wind. Because they can't sail straight into the wind, they zigzag upwind, going a little way on each tack.

It is important to have the boat moving along well, sailing close-hauled as you get ready to come about. Sing out, "ready about," to let your crew know you are about to tack over, then say "hard-a-lee" as you push the tiller to leeward. Leave the sheet right where it is set while the bow steers across the wind, until the sail fills on the other side. When you come about, the boat will heel over to the opposite side so the crew will want to change over to sit on the high side again.

The other way to change the boat's direction from one tack to the other is to *gybe*. When you gybe, you pull the tiller toward the windward side in order to steer the boat so the stern goes across the wind. As the boat gybes, the wind will catch the back of the sail and swing it across the boat pretty fast, so you must be careful.

Prepare for the gybe while you are sailing along on a broad reach, with the sail slacked out. Then gradually pull the tiller to windward to sail farther downwind. When the wind is coming over the stern of the boat, pull the sail in as you steer the stern across the wind. The wind will catch the back of the sail and push it out on the other side, so you must be ready to let the sheet run out quickly! Everyone should duck his or her head, too, when the sail comes across the boat.

Gybing is really easy, but it takes good timing. You should start out by learning in light wind. It is the quickest way to turn the boat around, and once you have mastered the gybe it can be a very sporty maneuver. On a windy day it can be a fun and exciting move!

Practice Makes Perfect

Once you have mastered tacking, gybing, and the other points of sail, continue practicing until you can do all the maneuvers smoothly in calm conditions and when the wind is blowing, too. It really is exciting to handle a sailboat in a good stiff breeze. But remember, a good captain is always cautious. Until you are really comfortable on all points of sail, start by sailing upwind so it will be easier to sail back downwind to the dock when you want to. Also, take a careful look at the weather before you go out sailing and don't sail too far from shore.

One of the best things about sailing is that you can never know everything about it. There is always something else to learn. Once you have mastered dinghy sailing, you can go on to bigger boats with mainsails and jibs. In competition, you fly spinnakers—huge balloonlike sails—when the boats sail downwind. The largest racing boats, the Maxis, are up to 85 feet long, with masts over a hundred feet high. They have over twenty in crew, and some race all the way around the world!

7 / Small Outboard Boats

There are two basic types of small outboard boats. They have either *displacement* or *planing* hulls. Displacement boats are the heavier type, with narrow sterns. As these boats move forward, the water flows around the boat. It is pushed aside by the bow, then it fills in behind the stern. Displacement boats can move only as fast as their length and shape allow the water to flow around them.

Planing boats generally are lighter and have wide sterns. At slow speeds they, too, push the water aside and it flows around them. But as planing boats go faster, they actually lift up and skim across the top of the water. This is called planing. When a runabout is planing, only a small area near the stern of the boat is still touching the water. The speed of planing boats is limited only by their seaworthiness and the amount of horsepower that is driving them. All racing type power-boats are of the planing type. Some go over a hundred miles per hour!

Outboards

The first lesson aboard small outboard boats involves becoming acquainted with the outboard itself. The outboard motor is clamped on to the *transom* of the boat. Start by making sure the clamps are tight. Usually, they are made up of two screw clamps with large tightening handles. Turn them clockwise to make sure they are tight.

It is also important for you to become familiar with the fuel system, starting cord, gearshift, and throttle. Many outboards also have a reverse lock, to keep them from lifting out of the water in reverse. All have a small *choke* lever that you pull out to help start the engine when it is cold. Although this sounds like a lot to learn, outboards are really easy to operate.

On small outboards, the fuel tank is located right on top of the engine. This makes it easy, because all you have to do is turn on the fuel valve on the side of the engine and open the vent at the top of the tank. Then the fuel flows into the motor by gravity. Larger outboards have a separate fuel tank. These are connected to the outboard by a rubber fuel line that plugs into the motor. Usually there is a vent on the fuel tank that must be opened to let the fuel flow. Also, there is a pump in the fuel line, an egg-shaped ball that you squeeze a few times to get the fuel up to the motor.

Once the fuel line is connected, or turned on, take a look at the right side of the outboard. This is where the gearshift lever is located. Most gearshift levers have three positions: forward, reverse, and neutral. Usually, you shift into forward by pulling the lever to the forward position. Neutral is at center, and reverse is with the lever pushed all the way back. For starting, the shift lever *always* should be set at neutral.

Both the steering and throttle usually are controlled by the same handle, which folds down from the outboard motor. The handle acts as a lever which turns the motor from side to side for steering control. Most throttles are located at the end of the handle, which twists, setting the speed from slow to fast. Many of the throttle controls will be labeled *stop, shift, start,* and *fast.*

The reverse lock usually is located just above the motor clamps, right where the motor is attached to the boat. The reverse lock always should be engaged when operating the outboard in all but very shallow water.

Getting Started

Once you are familiar with the outboard, you can start it up. The steps are easy to follow:

1. *Open the fuel valve and open the fuel tank vent. If there is a separate fuel tank, attach the fuel line and squeeze the egg-shaped fuel pump a few times.*
2. *Set the reverse lock in the* lock *position.*
3. *Set the gearshift in* neutral.
4. *Set the throttle on* start.
5. *If the engine is cold, or hasn't been run for awhile, pull out the choke lever for the first couple of pulls on the starting cord.*
6. *Give the starting cord a sharp pull to start the engine. Sometimes it takes two or three pulls to get the engine going.*
7. *As soon as the engine starts, push in the choke lever.*

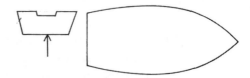

DISPLACEMENT HULLS:
NARROW STERN, ROUNDED BOTTOM.

PLANING HULLS:
WIDER AT TRANSOM, FLAT BOTTOM.

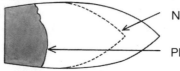

NORMAL WATERLINE

PLANING SURFACE

Getting Underway

With the engine running, you are ready to get underway. The easiest way to move your boat clear of the dock and any other boats is just to give the boat a shove out toward open water. When the boat is in clear water, shift into forward. You will feel the boat begin to move forward and you are underway!

Steering the outboard is easy. Using the steering handle, try turning the engine from side to side. As you move the motor, the propeller thrust is turned, which pushes the stern to the side you turn the motor. Spend some time getting used to the way your boat handles under power. See how tightly she'll turn in one direction and the other while powering along at a slow speed. Then slow the boat down and put her in neutral to see how far she coasts. This is called checking the boat's *carry*. It is very useful to know when you are making landings because you have to time it so the boat coasts gradually to the dock. Also get used to way the boat handles in reverse. It is good practice and lots of fun to see just how the boat reacts to your commands at the helm.

High-Speed Operation

Once you are comfortable operating the boat at low speeds, you are ready to move up to high speed. On a calm day without too much traffic, take the boat out and "open her up." A displacement boat will move along a good bit faster than before, and you'll enjoy moving about so quickly on the water. It is quite a thrill when a planing boat planes off and begins skimming across the water. Suddenly, the water's

resistance will seem to disappear and the boat will take off like a scared rabbit. In either type of boat, high-speed turns should be very gradual. Just turn the motor a tiny bit for an easy arc of a turn. Sharp turns at high speeds can be very dangerous, except with an expert boatman at the helm.

Powering around on the water in a runabout is a fun and exciting water sport. It's just like having a go-cart on land. You no longer have to row or paddle—the motor does the work for you as you cruise along, free to enjoy the scenery and the ride.

A Few Safety Tips

Although outboard boats offer some of the most enjoyable water transportation, there are a few safety rules that must be followed to keep you from getting into trouble.

1. *There must be a life jacket on the boat for everyone aboard. Wear them!*
2. *Always take a paddle or a set of oars in case the outboard breaks down.*
3. *Before getting underway, always check the fuel level to be sure you have enough fuel for the trip.*
4. *Never stand up in a moving powerboat. Not only do you risk falling overboard, but standing up makes the boat much more tippy.*
5. *Be careful in shallow water. If the propeller hits bottom it could break the shear pin. This can be fixed in time, but it will wreck your day on the water.*
6. *Be extremely careful around swimmers. The propeller could cause someone to be hurt very badly if it even touched them while it is spinning.*
7. *Be sure to slow down for big waves so the bow doesn't just plow into them and swamp the boat.*

If you always follow these safety rules, you are in for lots of fun times out there on the water. As you get used to operating powerboats, perhaps you will try water-skiing some day and driving the boat for the water-skiier. If you get the chance, take a ride with a skilled boatman in a real high-powered speedboat for the thrill of your life!

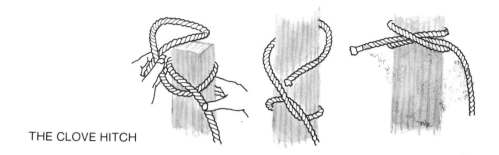

THE CLOVE HITCH

8 / Knots

One of the most common items aboard any boat is rope, or *line*, as we call it on the water. All small boats have a *painter* at the bow that is used to tie the boat to the dock. There is usually an anchor line aboard and several other small lines that are used for tying any loose gear to the boat. On sailboats, there is also the *sheet* for controlling the sail and the *halyard*, which hauls it up the mast. With all these lines aboard small boats, it is important to know how to tie good knots.

The most important thing a knot should do is to hold tight without slipping. The next most important thing is for the knot to come untied when you want it to. It is surprising how easily a knot can get stuck after it has been pulled really hard. This is the reason why sailors have developed special knots that are used on boats.

The basic knots for boating are the *clove hitch*, the *square knot*, the *bowline*, and the *figure eight* around a cleat. Look closely at the diagram for each kind of knot. You will see that they are really easy to tie. Practice each knot with a piece of clothesline or other spare line until you can do each knot quickly.

The Clove Hitch

The clove hitch is one of the easiest knots to tie. You just wrap the line around the post two times, passing the end underneath each wrap as you go around. Once you get the knack, the clove hitch is really fast to tie. It is used mostly for tying the boat's painter to a post on the dock when you come alongside.

41

SQUARE KNOT

The Square Knot

The square knot is also easy to tie. You start out with the two ends of the line, just like your shoelaces when you are tying your shoes. Pass one line over the other and pull tight in an *overhand knot*, like the beginning of a shoe knot. Remember which side you started with and do the same kind of overhand knot again. Pass the starting side over the other side and pull tight. That's all there is to it. You'll know if you tied a square knot because it will look just the same on the top and bottom. If the knot isn't the same on both sides, then you have tied a *granny knot*. "Grannies" hold well enough, but they sure are hard to untie if they are pulled tight.

Square knots are very handy for tying things together securely.

The Bowline

The bowline is a knot that is used for making a loop at the end of a line. It is one of the most popular boating knots because it never slips, and even if you pull with thousands of pounds the bowline is simple to untie.

Start the bowline by making a small circle with the line, near the end. Then just pull the end of the line up through the circle, around the line, and back down the same circle. There is a saying that will help you to remember the bowline. "The rabbit comes up the hole (the circle), around the tree (the line), and back down the hole (the circle).

BOWLINE

Practice the bowline a few times with clothesline and compare it with the diagram. You'll know when you've got it right.

The bowline has a great number of uses on boats. You can use it to tie the anchor line to the anchor, the sheets to the sail, or a tow-rope to a water-ski boat. The bowline is truly the boatman's knot.

The Cleat Knot

Many things on all types of boats are tied to cleats. A *cleat* is a metal fitting that is bolted to the boat. Then the line is wrapped around and around the cleat in the shape of a figure eight. This knot is also simple to learn. Anyone who knows what an eight looks like can tie one. Just wrap the line around the cleat, then across the cleat, and around the other side. Then do the same thing one more time. Finish the knot by wrapping the line all the way around the cleat one more time.

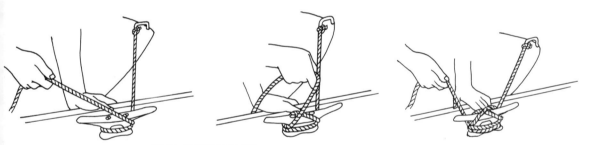

THE CLEAT KNOT

Cleats are used on sailboats for tying the *halyards* to hold the sails up and also for tying the main sheet when you are tired of trimming the sail by hand. They are sometimes used to tie the *painter* to the boat, and most of the time docks have them for boats to tie to.

If you learn these four knots, you will know the right knot for almost anything that has to be tied on boats. Each of these knots is easy and quick to tie, they hold tight, and you can untie them easily. Even just knowing this much will make you valuable crew on almost any boat!

9 / Seamanship

Seamanship is the art of doing things safely on boats. You don't have to be a crusty old sailor to be a good seaman. All you have to do is always use good judgment. Boats are no place for horseplay, because they are so much fun anyway. Just remember to be careful and have a good time!

Watch the Weather

Each time you go out in your boat, check the weather first. If it is starting to get cloudy and the wind is picking up, it might be better to wait for another day. It is no fun to get caught out in heavy weather in a small boat. If the wind is blowing hard away from the shore, be sure to stay very close in, so you don't get blown too far from the beach.

Be a Navigator

The navigator is the one who keeps track of where the boat is at all times. He or she makes sure the boat doesn't run aground in shallow water and always keeps track of how to get back to the dock. Experienced navigators are very good at recording the boat's position even when they are out of sight of land or when it is very foggy. Navigation is a science in itself. The best way to start is to pay close attention to the landmarks near your destination and at your home base while someone else is navigating.

Don't Forget the Safety Gear

Every boat should have enough life preservers for everyone aboard, and everyone on the boat should wear one. It is also very important to carry a spare paddle or oar in all boats. If you run out of gas in a small outboard runabout or if the wind dies while you are out sailing, you will be glad to have a paddle aboard. Then you can paddle back to the dock. All boats should have a bailer or a bilge pump to pump out any water that leaks in. There should be an anchor and anchor line, too, in case you have to stop the boat for any reason.

Stay With the Boat!

If the boat ever did tip over, the most important thing to remember is to stay with the boat. Even upside down, most boats will stay afloat, so all you have to do is hold on until help arrives. In some boating classes, one of the lessons is to tip the boat over in shallow water near the beach. Then the instructor can show you how to "right" the boat and prepare it for the return trip to shore. The first thing you learn in this lesson is that it is OK to swim around the boat as you gather up the gear and prepare the boat to be towed in. But it is important to stay close to the boat so you can hold on and float with it.

Anyone Can Be a Good Seaman

A good seaman is one of the most respected men on the waterfront. He knows many different things about boats and the sea. He understands the weather and is a good judge of when it is safe to go out in his boat. He is a good navigator. He always knows where he is when he is out there on the water and how to get back. He knows his boat well enough to fix most things if something breaks. A seaman also carries plenty of safety gear, such as life jackets, bilge pumps, flashlights, and a first-aid kit. Also, he knows how his boat handles and never operates it unsafely. The best seamen aren't afraid of the ocean but they respect it. They go out in their boats well prepared.

10 / Getting Started

Boating has become so popular that you can find boats to learn on almost anywhere. Even inland, far from the ocean, there are all types of small boats on lakes and rivers. If you want to learn about boats, you shouldn't have to travel too far!

The National Red Cross teaches courses in small-boat handling. They also have special classes for sailing and canoeing.

The YM–YWCA and YM–YWHA teach boating in many of their summer camps. Most other summer camps also have boating classes where you can get started.

Many city parks rent rowboats and canoes on the park lakes. All you have to do is call the city park department to find out if and where boats are available for rent. Many cities also have good boating classes where you can learn all the basics.

Also, try asking your school librarian or gym teacher how to go about finding a place to begin boating.

Any local marina or boat-launching area is another good place to go for information on how to get out on the water. Most boating people are friendly and helpful. If you really want to learn about boats, you probably will find that it is easy to get good suggestions around the boat docks.

As you become involved with boating, you will find that it is a hobby that can bring a lifetime of fun and adventure. So, welcome aboard! Enjoy yourself out there on the water!

Glossary

Athwartship—Across the boat, or side to side.

Bear off—Steer away from the wind.

Blade—The flat, wide section at the base of an oar.

Boom—A pole coming back from a sailboat's mast that holds the bottom edge of the sail.

Bow—The front of a boat.

Broad reaching—Sailing with the wind a little behind you.

Carry—The ability of a boat to coast through the water.

Centerboard—A foil-shaped board located in the middle of a sailboat that keeps it from slipping sideways through the water.

Center of buoyancy—The center of a boat's underbody where the force of water pushing up is focused.

Center of gravity—The exact center of all the boat's weight.

Chafeguard—A strip of leather or other protective material used to protect any part of a boat from wearing as it rubs another part of the boat.

Choke lever—On outboard motors, a lever that is turned on to help the engine start when it is cold.

Closehauled—Sailing as close to the wind as possible.

Close reaching—Sailing a little bit into the wind but with the sail let out slightly.

Come about—Turning a sailboat's bow across the wind to change direction.

Displacement—The total weight of a boat. This equals the amount of water it pushes aside with its bottom.

Displacement boats—Boats that travel through the water, rather than skimming across the top of the water.

Downwind—Toward the direction the wind is traveling.

Feathering—Flattening the oar or paddle for the return stroke.

Gunnel, or Gunwale—The top edges on both sides of a boat.

Gybe—Turning a sailboat's stern across the wind to change direction.

Head up—Turn into the wind.

Heel—When a sailboat tips to leeward because of pressure on the sail.

J Stroke—A paddling stroke in the shape of a J, used to keep a canoe going straight.

Keel—The center plank, or "backbone," of a wooden boat. Also, a deep fin on a sailboat that keeps it from being blown sideways.

Leeward—Toward the downwind side of the boat.

Loom—The inside portion of an oar, from the oarlock to the handle.

Luffing—When the sail flaps in the breeze.

Mast—A tall spar that supports the sails on all sailboats.

Oarlock—A pivoting fitting that holds an oar in place.

Planing hulls—Boats that can ride up and skim across the top of the water.

Port—The left side of a boat.

Portage—Carrying a canoe overland to another river or lake.

Reaching—Sailing across the wind.

Running—Sailing in the same direction as the wind is blowing.

Sheet—The line that is used for controlling a boat's sail.

Starboard—The right side of a boat.

Stern—The back end of a boat.

Stern pry—Using the paddle like a rudder to steer a canoe.

Stern sweep—A paddling stroke in the shape of an arc, in toward the paddler.

Tack—Turning a sailboat's bow across the wind to change direction.

Tiller—The lever, or arm, coming forward from a boat's rudder that is used for steering control.

Transom—The section that is squared off at the extreme back edge of a boat.

Upwind—In the direction the wind is coming from.

Windward—The side of a boat that is closer to the wind.

Index